SUMMARY OF 18 MAHA PURANAS

BRIEF ABOUT THE 18 MAHAPURANAS

DR. JAGADEESH PILLAI

Made with ♥ on the Notion Press Platform
www.notionpress.com

!! Dedicated to all seekers of Spiritual Wisdom !!

Contents

Contents

Prayer

Oṃ bhūr bhuvaḥ suvaḥ
Tat savitur vareṇyaṃ
Bhargo devasya dhīmahi
Dhiyo yo naḥ prachodayāt

About The Author Of This Book

Dr. Jagadeesh Pillai, a four-time Guinness World Record holder, voracious reader, writer, and true research scholar, was born in Varanasi, the abode of Lord Shiva. He holds a Ph.D. in Vedic Science and is a multi-faceted polymath with innate qualities, creative ideas, and remarkable achievements. Although his roots extend back to Kerala, the residents of Varanasi feel proud of him and adore him as a child of Varanasi who selflessly caters to those in need. A deep study of his profile reveals that he has added many feathers to his cap, making him quite unique. His four Guinness World Records are in the following subjects:

1. "Script to Screen" which he achieved by producing and directing a state of art animation film within the shortest time possible by breaking the earlier set record by Canadians. There are many national and international Awards and Recognitions to his credit.
2. Longest Line of Post Cards which he has done on the occasion of 163 years of Indian Postal Day by 16300 post cards. The event was also connected with a questionnaire about Indian Flag.
3. Largest Poster Awareness Campaign – This was achieved by designing an awareness campaign on the subject "Beti Bachao – Beti Padhao".
4. Largest Envelop – Towards tribute to Prime Minister's initiative 'Make in India' – he has created about 4000 sq meter envelop using waste papers.
5. Attempted by lighting 70000 candles on a 210 kg cake to celebrate the 70th Indian Independence day recorded in World Records India.

6. Attempted a documentary on Dhamek Stupa of Sarnath dubbing in 17 languages, result is waiting from Guinness World Records.

He is versatile in Gita teaching. The young generation is fond of his Gita teaching and he has changed the life of many young through his continued motivational boost up and teachings.

He has composed and sung hundreds of Sanskrit Bhajans, Patriotic songs, etc.

He has written and directed so many short films and documentaries for awareness campaigns.

He has done voluntary services to UP Police and Kerala Police to spread awareness campaigns on the various issue through videos and photography.

He is on the path of authoring thousands of books on Indian culture, Indian Temples, and the life of extraordinary people.

It is hard to believe that he has produced and directed more than 100 Documentaries on a particular city (Varanasi) which is done by a single person.

He has helped and guided more than 25 boys and girls to achieve world records through various creative and innovative methods.

A multifaceted person who can apply the best of his intellect using the God-given blessings which have been showered upon every human being granting them an immense capacity to learn, experience, and experiment with many things and do wonders in this world of discrimination and disparities.

He is a teacher and a student at the same time who always learns every day and teaches every day. As a master, his weakness was that he never sticks to a particular subject. Perhaps this weakness gives him the strength to master any area which he came across.

Each of his days dawned with learning a new topic and he spend most of his time experimenting and researching it.

He is also a selfless social activist and a motivational speaker.

His life was full of struggle, ups and downs, and failures. But he never gave up and faced all his trials and tribulations full of confidence. Today he is a successful young man with a lot of enthusiasm and rich life experience.

He is an efficient Tarot Card Reader, Astro-Vastu Consultant and an excellent singer and composer.

He has sung full Ram Charita Manas 138 hours audio by his own composition. He has also sung the whole Bhagavad-Gita in his own composition with a rhythmic background.

He has also sung "Lokah Samastha Sukhino Bhavantu" in 50 different languages.

Currently working on a detailed and scientific study on

Veda, Upanishad, Puranas, Bhagavad Gita, etc.

He has composed and sung Hanuman Chalisa in 108 different compositions and Gayatri Mantra in 1008 different compositions.

Awards

Four Times Guinness World Records, Winner of Mahatma Gandhi Vishwa Shanti Puraskar, Mahatma Gandhi Global Peace Ambassador, Kashi Ratna Award, Dr. APJ Abdul Kalam Motivational Person of the Year 2017, Mother Teresa Award, Indira Gandhi Priyadarshini Award, Bharat Vikas Ratna Award, Udyog Ratna Award, Vigyan Prasar Award, Poorvanchal Ratn Samman etc.

Preface

The 18 Puranas are a collection of ancient Hindu religious texts, and constitute a significant portion of Hindu scripture. This book aims to give a concise overview of these texts and their relevance to modern Hinduism.

The 18 Puranas are divided into three distinct categories. The first group, consisting of the Vishnu Purana, Shiv Purana, Padma Purana, and Varaha Purana, focus mainly on the worship of the gods Vishnu, Shiva, and Brahma, and detail their avatars and numerous deeds. The second category comprises the Bhagavata Purana, Narada Purana, Garuda Purana, Kurma Purana, and Skanda Purana; these contain the life stories of important figures such as Krishna, the son of Vishnu, and his numerous incarnations. The third category consists of the Matsya Purana, Agni Purana, Linga Purana, Brahmanda Purana, Markandeya Purana, Vayu Purana, Brahma Purana, and Bhavisya Purana. This group is mainly concerned with detailing the creation of the universe, the development of Hinduism and Indian culture, and proper conduct for Hindus.

These texts have a long and complex history, as evidenced by their numerous translations over the centuries. The earliest versions of the Puranas are thought to have originated between 400 BCE and 200 CE; later versions have been penned as recently as the early 19th century. During this time period, the Puranas underwent several revisions and adaptations to suit the changing needs and sensibilities of the Hindu people.

The Puranas are typically written in Sanskrit, the primary language of Hindu religious texts, though some sections are written in other languages. Each convey a clear religious message, and their primary purpose is to glorify God and instruct the reader in the correct way of worship and living. A closely related text is the Ramayana, an epic poem about the life of the god Rama and his battle against the demon king Ravana. These two texts are closely intertwined, with the Ramayana often referenced in the Puranas, and the Puranas sometimes retold as a part of the Ramayana.

The 18 Puranas represent a vast wealth of knowledge about Hinduism and serve as a source of valuable information on its culture and practices. They are a fundamental part of Hinduism and are widely used in both private and public life. Thus, this book seeks to give a concise overview of these texts and explain their importance in Hinduism. It also provides a way to better understand and appreciate the different kinds of Hindu literature.

CHAPTER ONE

ORIGIN OF PURANA

The Sanskrit word 'Pura' and 'Ana' are combined to form the term 'Purana', which literally translates to 'ancient' or 'ancient times'. The word 'Pura' means 'unseen' and 'past', while 'Ana' means 'to speak or narrate'. Puranas are believed to be the oldest religious texts, which were first created by the creator Brahma. They contain ancient facts, theories, teachings, ethics, laws, and events. Puranas are considered to be the oldest literature in the world and still contain valuable knowledge and morality that serve as the foundation of modern and human society.

CHAPTER TWO

About the Author of Puranas

The author of the 18 Puranas is Vedavyasa, also known as Krishna Dwaipayana. Along with these Puranas, some other Upapuranas were also created during the transition period, and the number of Upapuranas kept increasing. However, when it comes to the authorship of the original Puranas, all of them are attributed to the divine Vedavyasa.

CHAPTER THREE

Introduction to 18 Maha Puranas

The eighteen Puranas are ancient Hindu texts which are considered to be part of the Hindu Smriti (sacred texts). These texts contain stories, instructions, and explanations of various aspects of Hinduism. The Puranas, together with the Vedas and Upanishads, form the major text of Hinduism. The eighteen Puranas are all of equal authority, although there is great variety in their contents.

Vishnu Purana - was composed by Sage Parashara. Its protagonist is Lord Vishnu, who is the source of creation, eternity, imperishability, non-duality, and unity. This scripture contains detailed descriptions of the measurements of the elements such as the sky, the measurements of the celestial bodies such as the sea and the sun, the origin of the gods, the divisions of the universe, the complete Dharma and the characters of the sages and the rishis.

Shiva Purana - Lord Shiva has been described in detail with his various forms, avatars, lingams, devotees, and devotion. This includes a philosophical interpretation of Shiva's benevolent form, mysteries, glory, and worship.

Padma Purana - which is composed of five books. It deals with topics such as Karma and its results, the virtues and vices of people, and the methods of worshiping Lord Vishnu.

Varaha Purana - which is composed of twenty-four thousand verses. It contains descriptions of many sacred places as well as instructions on religious acts and ceremonies. The Purana contains two stories about the Boar Avatar.

Bhagavata Purana - which is written in the form of a dialogue between Sage Sukha and Lord Krishna. It contains descriptions of various physical worlds and other cosmic aspects, discussions of various yogas and their applications, and narrates stories of various characters in the Mahabharata.

Narada Purana - a classical text that narrates the tales of the god Vishnu. It is divided into two parts and covers various topics including cosmology, Vedic rituals, theology, and philosophy. This Purana offers insights into the various aspects of life such as birth and death, justice, and sin and virtue.

Garuda Purana - which is a Vaishnava scripture that primarily focuses on the story of the bird-god Garuda. It contains important information about shastras, astrology, and other sacred texts. It can also provide guidance on ethical living as it has several references to the importance of spiritual power and moral integrity.

Kurma Purana - it is believed to be one of the most ancient Puranas. This scripture deals mostly with legends and mythology, but there are also many aspects of spiritual and ethical living described within its chapters. It contains the Sun's race with the demon Tarakasura, the churning of the ocean, and the famous story of Ramachandra.

Skanda Purana - it concentrates on the life and teachings of Lord Shiva. It is believed to be the longest of all the Puranas and considers topics such as cosmology, theology, philosophy, astrology, and mythology. With condensed explanations in the text about the gods of the Hindu pantheon, this Purana also offers detailed guidance on important rites and rituals.

Vamana Purana - The text is largely devoted to detailing Lord Vishnu's fifth avatar, Vamana, who was born in response to a curse inflicted by King Mahabali. It includes stories and teachings that shed light on many important aspects of Hindu faith and practices such as yoga, meditation, astrology, vegetarianism and sacred rites.

Matsya Purana - it is among the oldest and most important of the Puranas. This scripture dates back to the first millennium BCE, and it contains information about the origin of the universe. It describes the creation of the world, the story of Manu, the ancestral king of mankind, and the story of the great flood. The Matsya Purana is also a source of knowledge about Vedic cosmology and the importance of yajnas for the removal of negative karma.

Agni Purana - which is in the form of a dialogue between Sage Agastya and King Yudhishthira about preparations for a great yajna, or sacrifice. It contains details on rituals, astrology, geography, narrates stories of gods, goddesses as well as legendary kings and heroes.

Linga Purana - which is in the form of a dialogue between the gods Shiva and Vishnu. It contains detailed descriptions of Shivalingas, narrates the shrines and holy places in India, and provides instructions on rituals related to the worship of Shiva.

The Brahmanda Purana - also known as the "Great Purana", is one of the most important, containing a wealth of information on the history of India and the many great kings and their wars, as well as their contributions to the world. This Purana also focuses heavily on philosophical aspects such as karma and the importance of following the Dharma Code in all aspects of life.

Markandeya Purana - which is in the form of a dialogue between Sage Markandeya and the god Shiva. It contains discussions on the origin and end of the universe, the duties of man, and principles of morality.

The Brahmavaivarta Purana - also known as the Vaishnava Purana, contains descriptions of the characters of Lord Ganesha, Lakshmi, Savitri, and Lord Krishna. It also contains knowledge of Ayurveda.

Brahma Purana - is an ancient Indian encyclopedic treatise that contains a wealth of information on cosmology, genealogy (including the solar dynasty), mythology, geology, and Dharma (the universal law of nature). It is a comprehensive source of knowledge that has been passed down through the ages, providing insight into the culture and beliefs of ancient India.

The Bhavisya Purana - is primarily focused on the future of the universe and the future incarnations of Hindu gods, as well as the instances in which they will have to descend to the earth. This Purana also focuses on the importance of Deva worship, especially during difficult times.

These scriptures are full of ancient spiritual knowledge and stories that continue to influence the world today. They cover topics such as ritual, cosmology, mythology and even psychology. For those already familiar with Hindu spiritual concepts, these puranas offer a wealth of knowledge for further insight and growth.

CHAPTER FOUR

Sloka for Easy Identification of Puranas

Memorizing a Sanskrit shloka will help you to remember all the names of Puranas.

"ma-dwayam bha-dwayam chaiva bra-thrayam va-chathushtayam
anapalinga kooska-ni puranani prudhak prudhak"

Meaning:

Ma two times (Matsya and Markendeya)
Bha two times (Bhagavata and Bhavishya)
Bra three times (Brahma, Brahmanda, Brahma Vraivrata)
Va four times (Vayu, Vamana, Varaha, Vishnu)
A-na-pa-lin-ga (Agni, Narada, Padma, Linga, Garuda)
Koo-ska (Kurma, Skanda)

CHAPTER FIVE

Classification Per Gunas

Sattva (Truth)

Shiva Purana, Linga Purana, Vishnu Purana, Bhagavata Purana, Naradeya Purana, Garuda Purana, Brahmanda Purana, Padma Purana, and Varaha Purana.

Rajas (Passion)

Markandeya Purana, Bhavishya Purana, Brahma Vaivarta Purana, Vamana Purana and Brahma Purana.

Tamas (Ignorance)

Matsya, Kurma, Skanda, and Agni Purana.

FIRST GROUP

The first group, consisting of the Vishnu Purana, Shiv Purana, Padma Purana, and Varaha Purana, focus mainly on the worship of the gods Vishnu, Shiva, and Brahma, and detail their avatars and numerous deeds.

CHAPTER SIX

Vishnu Purana

The Vishnu Purana is an ancient Hindu sacred text dating to the 5th century CE. It emphasize different aspects of the divine life, lessons, and mantras. The first volume focuses on creation stories, cosmology and philosophy, providing insights into how Hindus view their place in the universe. The second volume is devoted to descriptions of many avatars of Vishnu—one way to visualize aspects of God's energy—and emphasizes devotion to him as supreme deity. The third volume offers moral guidance for individuals and society, taught through stories from various incarnations like Rama, Krishna and Kalki. Additionally it closes with a section that describes mantra-based meditation practices used to train the mind for spiritual growth. The fourth book deals with rituals that are geared toward achieving liberation from bondage in this world and attaining union with Brahman (God). Finally the fifth volume consists of genealogies and mythology related particularly by Vishnu's dynasty. All these components together offer deeper understanding into the life-enabling beliefs that constitute Hinduism while providing techniques to refine one's consciousness on its path towards communicating with God directly.

A few of the key themes and lessons contained in the Vishnu Purana are the importance of ethics and Dharma, the power of selfless devotion, the rewards of attaining Moksha or liberation through right action, the proper performance of rituals, and the practice of meditation. In addition to these lessons, there are also many spiritual mantras contained in the text, like the famous Vishnu Sahasranama (which extols the thousand names of Lord Vishnu) and other mantras used to invoke Vishnu and his divine qualities.

The Vishnu Purana also has many poems and hymns which provide further spiritual guidance from the grace of Lord Vishnu. One such powerful mantra is:

"Om Namo Bhagavate Vasudevaya
Namah Shivaya Cha Mahadevaya
Namo Vishnave Prabhuve Namaste Vayu
Namah Narayanaya Devadaya Namaha"

Another famous mantra from the Vishnu Purana is the "Namaskar" mantra, which reads:

"Om Namo Narayanaya Namaha Om Namo Vasudevaya Namaha
Om Namo Vishnave Namaha Om Namo Shivaya Namaha
Om Namo Brahmane Namaha Om Namo Madhusudanaya Namaha"

The Vishnu Purana consists of six sections, with a total of 126 chapters, 23,000 or 24,000 or 6,000 verses. The author of this scripture is Sage Parashara and the listener is Maitreya.

It includes stories of Lord Vishnu, his incarnation Balarama, and Krishna Avatar. Additionally, it also includes the story of King Prahlada, which is why our planet is called Pṛthvi. This scripture also contains the history of the Suryavanshi and Chandravanshi kings. India's national identity has been ancient for centuries, which is evident in the following verse from the Vishnu Purana: "Uttaram Yat Samudrasya Himadreshchaiva Dakshinam". (In simple words, this means that the geographical area surrounded by the Himalayas in the north and the ocean in the south is known as Bharat, and all the people living in it are descendants of Bharat). What could be a clearer identification of India and Indians than this? The Vishnu Purana is truly an historic scripture.

CHAPTER SEVEN

Shiv Purana

The Shiva Purana is an important Hindu text that focuses on the worshiping of Lord Shiva. It contains stories, mantras, lessons and myths related to this deity and acts as a guide in understanding the concept of God through faith. It can also provide spiritual guidance to those seeking answers from within their souls. The primary themes of the Shiva Purana include Shiva's philosophy, his forms as well as other deities, his manifestations, and associated stories. Additionally, devotees learn about rituals for personal transformation and how to live life according to God's teachings. This work also discusses various mantras for chanting during prayer or meditation; these are said to be prayers for protection, wisdom, peace and inner bliss. Ultimately the Shiva Purana provides one with a greater understanding of devotion to Lord Shiva which allows them to find liberation from suffering in life.

The Shiva Purana is one of the most important Hindu texts. It is considered to be part of the Shaivism tradition and venerates Lord Shiva as the Supreme Lord. The Purana is full of stories, teachings, and mantras related to Shiva, his worship and all aspects of Shiva's life, works and naatures.

Out of eighteen major Puranas in Hinduism , the Shiva Purana ranks as one of the most important in the set. It is divided into seven books with five chapters each. This Purana is focused on the teachings regarding Shiva and his worship. Its contents include stories of the various incarnations of Lord Shiva, homage to the gods, conquering of the demons, legends of Shiva's ascetics and devotees, and the setting of temple rules.

The stories in this text teach the importance of self-realisation, and speak to the power of Lord Shiva as the transcendental and divine power and the ultimate teacher. It also encourages spiritual practices such as yoga, nama-japa (chanting the name of Shiva), scapular and lingam worship. The Shiva Purana also provides summarised version of other scriptures like the Mahabharata, Ramayana and Bhagavata Purana.

An important lesson from this text is that all the dualities of life can be dissolved through Shiva, who is the ultimate goal of life and the source of all auspiciousness. It also outlines the importance of having faith and devotion to Lord Shiva, and explains that only through such devotion can one gain insight into the mysteries of the world. Furthermore, the text also explains how to perform worship of Shiva, including detailed instructions on how to perform puja rituals, how to chant various mantras, and how to make offerings to Lord Shiva.

The Shiva Purana also contains an impressive selection of mantras that are said to be used in meditation and spiritual practices. These mantras are used to invoke the divine power of Shiva, praise his greatness and make him the centre of one's existence. Some key mantras include the Mahamritunjaya Mantra, Shiva Panchakshari, Shri Rudram, Maha Mrityunjaya, Maha Mrityunjaya Beej Mantra, Shiva Gayatri Mantra, and many more.

The Shiv Puran contains 24,000 shlokas and is divided into seven samhitas. This text describes the greatness of Lord Shiva and the events related to him. (It is also known as the Vayu Purana or a part of it). It includes descriptions of the Kalash Parvat, Shivling, and Rudraksha, the creation of the names of the days of the week, the description of the Prajapatis and their victory over Kam. The names of the days of the week are based on the planets of our solar system and are still used in almost the entire world today.

To sum up, the Shiva Purana is a comprehensive text of Hinduism and provides invaluable insight into Shiva and his worship. It is full of stories, mantras and lessons that offer a powerful reminder of the truths of life and our relationship to the divine. Through its teachings and mantras, it helps to cultivate a deeper connection with Shiva and to find true happiness and enlightenment.

CHAPTER EIGHT

Padma Purana

The Padma Purana is one of the eighteen major Hindu texts and is known for containing many stories, mantras, and teachings related to Vishnu. In terms of structure, the biblical-type text has five main parts: Virata Parva (on creation), Bhumikanda (on cosmic journeys), Kriyayogasara (on meditation), Uttarakhanda (on Buddhism) and Patala Khanda (on heavenly pleasures). Each section touches on different themes such as mantras, karma, faith in god, life after death, good vs. evil, devotion to Vishnu and more. Additionally, many of its stories serve as moral lessons and parables that teach Hindus about how to live a meaningful life on Earth. Finally, due to its comprehensive character it's often seen as an encyclopedia for Hindu worshipers seeking enlightenment.

Padma Purana is one of the eighteen traditional Puranas, which are ancient Indian texts. The Padma Purana is written in Sanskrit and contains a wealth of information about Hindu mythology, philosophy, and religious practices. It is one of the earliest documents accessible to modern scholars and is divided into five books or Khandas. Each of these chapters contains a variety of stories, myths, and teachings about both human and divine subjects.

The Padma Purana is one of the most important sources of texts related to Hinduism and is considered to be an authoritative source on the practice of Hindu worship. The Purana is believed to have been written in the first century CE, and is believed by Hindus to have been passed down to humanity through sages. It is not only one of the most important works of Indian literature but also serves as a guidebook for Hindu Sadhana or spiritual practice.

The Padma Purana is particularly important for its teachings on Yoga, Tantra, the worship of deities like Vishnu, Shiva, and Lakshmi, and the practice of Vratas or vows. The five khandas of the Padma Purana, Uttara Kanda, Bhumika, Patala, Skanda, and Srishti, contain over 55,000 verses. This immense volume contains stories, teachings, and lessons about righteousness, charity, honesty, and living in harmony with the environment.

The Padma Purana also contains an array of important rituals, both fervent and pacific, and mantras, which form a major part of the practice of Hinduism. According to the teachings of the Purana, these teachings and mantras can help one in physical, mental, and spiritual advancement. In addition to the mantras and teachings, the Padma Purana includes instructions on the performance of many important Hindu ceremonies and rituals, such as Ganesha Puja and Varalakshmi Vrata.

The Padma Purana also features many ethical and spiritual lessons, especially related to the practice of devotion and worship. It emphasizes the importance of charity and virtue and encourages adherence to the path of goodness.

The Padma Purana further serves as guidance for Hindus in everyday life, prescribing a variety of practices and rituals for good health, luck, and prosperity.

The Padma Purana contains 55,000 verses and is divided into five sections: Sristi Khand, Swarga Khand, Uttara Khand, Bhumi Khand, and Patala Khand. According to the Matsya Purana, there were 55,000 verses and according to the Brahma Purana, there were 59,000 verses. In total, the Padma Purana consists of 641 chapters and 48,000 verses. It was narrated by Suta Ugrashrava, the son of Lomaharshana. This text sheds light on many topics, including devotion to Vishnu in many forms. It is believed to have been developed in the 5th century.

The Padma Purana contains detailed descriptions of the creation of the Earth and the heavens, as well as the four types of creation of living beings: Udvibhaj, Svedaj, Andaj, and Jarayuja. This classification is scientifically accurate. It also provides an extensive description of all the mountains and rivers of India. The text also contains the history of many ancient figures, from Shakuntala Dushyanta to Lord Rama. It is said that Bharatkhand was named after Bharata, the son of Shakuntala Dushyanta, and later became India.

In sum, the impact of the Padma Purana is evident, as it is an important source of Hinduism's teachings, rituals, and mantras. It is a comprehensive and comprehensive collection of verses and teachings enshrined in Hindu mythology and spiritual practice. The Padma Purana is thus considered one of the most important and influential works of Hindu literature.

CHAPTER NINE

Varaha Purana

The Varaha Purana is one of the most ancient Hindu holy texts, written in Sanskrit during the 4th or 5th century A.D. It details the relationship between humanity and God, with a particular focus on Vishnu —one of the "preserver" gods of Hindu belief—and his incarnation as Varaha (the wild boar). The stories contained in this Purana feature several legendary characters, such as Bhagiratha and many others. In addition to these narratives, it also speaks of dozens of religious ceremonies, recitation of mantras, rules for purification and devotion. The core message of the book is the importance of strong attachment to God through selfless service and ritualistic practices. It emphasizes that those who revere Vishnu will ultimately achieve liberation from their earthly sufferings. So while this ancient scripture provides its readers with insights into metaphysical precepts, it also contains valuable life lessons about true selflessness and faithfulness to one's beliefs.

The Varaha Purana is an important ancient Hindu scripture, and is considered to be one of the eighteen major Puranas. It is said to be a part of the knowledge given by Lord Vishnu to the sage Pulastya, who then narrated it to the sage Parashar. The content of the text is written in

Sanskrit and dates back to the 5th century BCE. The text is divided into two parts; Purvaramba, which is the first part consisting of two sections and Uttararambha, which consists of the last three sections.

The text is primarily focused on doctrines, cosmogony and expounds the characteristics of various Hindu Gods and Goddesses, the teachings from philosophical schools of Hinduism, the five elements of nature (ether, air, fire, water, and earth), the duties and responsibilities of kings, the role of Brahmins, and the importance of performing sacrifices and worshiping Lord Vishnu.

The Varaha Purana is divided into three major books called the Adhyatma, the Udhbhava, and the Ubhaya. The Adhyatma explains the secrets and secrets of gods, goddesses, bestowing supremacy, and spiritual independence and the dispelling of sins. The Udhbhava book explains the aim of life and salvation attained through three-fold discipline, penance, purity and devotion. The Ubhaya book explains the importance of knowledge and meditation.

The Varaha Purana explains the importance of mantras, which are Sanskrit words that have a certain power and charm behind them. Mantras are seen as powerful vibrations that are capable of producing corresponding resonances; and when used with love and devotion may invoke the special energy of a deity or even the Supreme being. Examples of mantras from the Varaha Purana include the "Mahalakshmi Gayatri Mantra" which is one of the oldest and most powerful Hindu mantras devoted to Goddess Lakshmi; and the "Nrisimhastakam" which is a set of eight mantras devoted to Lord Vishnu.

The Varaha Purana is a rich source of knowledge and valuable lessons that have been passed down for centuries and still remain relevant today. Its message emphasizes correct living, the understanding of one's true nature, and becoming liberated from materialistic tendencies. It teaches us the importance of understanding the relationship between our actions and the results, of serving and helping others, and of looking at the divine in all things. In short, the Varaha Purana is a source of knowledge and spiritual guidance, and its teachings are sure to enrich and enlighten our lives.

The description in this is of Vishnu's avatar, Varaha. Varaha rescued the Earth from the netherworld and preached this scripture. It contains 24,000 shlokas and only 11,000 verses and 217 chapters.

In addition to the story of Varaha's avatar, this text also provides an extensive description of the Bhagavata Gita, Mahamaya. It also describes the creation, heaven, netherworld, and other worlds. It also mentions the Shraddha ritual, the northward and southward motion of the sun, the Amavasya and the full moon. What is remarkable is that the geographical and astronomical facts contained in this scripture were only discovered by Western scientists in the 19th century.

SECOND GROUP

The second category comprises the Bhagavata Purana, Narada Purana, Garuda Purana, Kurma Purana, Vamana Purana and Skanda Purana; these contain the life stories of important figures such as Krishna, the son of Vishnu, and his numerous incarnations.

CHAPTER TEN

Bhagavata Purana

The Bhagavata Purana is one of the most widely known and read Puranas. It is known as the source of all spiritual knowledge, "Nigamakalpataru", and the examination ground of the wise, "Vidyavatam Bhagavate Pariksha". It is devoted to the devotion of Lord Krishna and contains 12 Skandhas, 335 chapters, and 18,000 verses. Some scholars refer to it as the "Devi Bhagavata Purana" due to its detailed description of the divine (Shakti). It is believed to have been composed in the 6th century.

The Bhagavata Purana tell stories from Hindu mythology, centred on Lord Krishna. It provides guidance on moral and spiritual topics such as karma, dharma and devotion to God. Containing a collection of verses, it also includes mantras used for meditation and worship and teaches important lessons about love, compassion, peace and understanding. It further instructs readers on how to live with inner peace and tap into their divine consciousness. Its themes linger long after its closing words are read - invoking introspection in our minds towards the highest truth within us all.

The Bhagavata Purana is an ancient Hindu religious text,

written by the sage Vyasa in Sanskrit. It is one of the most important Hindu scriptures, and is also known as the Srimad Bhagavatam or the Bhagavad Puran. The Bhagavata Purana was written to expound the philosophy of Vaishnavism, and is considered by devotees to be the most popular of the Vedic texts.

The Bhagavata Purana is centered on Lord Krishna, who is revered as the supreme being in Hinduism. It narrates His life and many of His teachings and explores the various aspects of His miracles and spiritual powers. It comprises twelve volumes, each containing thousands of verses that teach about the ultimate nature of God, His divinity, and His untold greatness.

The Bhagavata Purana also contains a range of mantras that devotees use for contemplation and meditation. These verses, known as shlokas, are often chanted during puja ceremonies and religious functions. They provide devotees with a way of connecting to the divine and drawing spiritual energy from Him. Some of the most popular mantras found in the Bhagavata Purana include the Mahamantra, Hare Krishna, and the Vishnu Sahasranaam.

The Bhagavata Purana contains a wealth of lessons and moral precepts, especially when it comes to living a virtuous life. It teaches us to cultivate spiritual love and devotion to Lord Krishna, and to perform righteousness and good deeds in accordance with His will. Other important lessons include the importance of charity, inner beauty, and the futility of material possessions.

The Bhagavata Purana is a profound and timeless religious

work, and it is highly revered among Hindus. Its verses are filled with wisdom and provide devotees with great spiritual guidance. From its powerful mantras to its invaluable lessons and moral precepts, the Bhagavata Purana offers the path to a fulfilling life of devotion and contemplation.

This Purana is one of the most widely studied and read, as it focuses on Vaishnavism and Vishnu's avatars. It includes contentious dynasty-specific genealogy information, and there are numerous conflicting translations of this text as well as historical documents in other Indian languages. It is particularly important and developed during the Bhakti movement.

It is a dialogue on spiritual topics, glorifying the greatness of devotion, knowledge, and detachment. In addition to the stories of Vishnu and Krishna, it also includes tales of many kings, sages, and asuras from before the Mahabharata era. It also provides details of Krishna's death by sacrifice, the submergence of Dwarka, and the destruction of the Yadu dynasty. This text is a great source of knowledge and wisdom, and is a must-read for all spiritual seekers.

CHAPTER ELEVEN

Narada Purana

The Narada Purana is one of the eighteen major Hindu scriptures and is a compilation of various teachings from other texts. It consists of two parts- (a) Vaisnava section, which focuses on Vishnu and includes teachings about him; and (b) Shaiva section, which focuses on Shiva. The Purana covers many topics such as spiritual philosophy, cosmology, marriage customs, geography, genealogy, astrology, mathematics, devotional literature, Bhakti yoga practices etc. In terms of lessons and mantras derived from this scripture – it teaches us the importance of devotion to God without expectations or attachments; to be true to our faith; to lead virtuous lives so we may attain salvation; the power of mantra chanting and meditation in creating positive vibrations that help spread peace and blessings.

This ancient text is also known as the Mahapurana. It does not contain the five characteristics of a Purana. It describes the festivals and rituals of the Vaishnavas. It is divided into two parts: (a) the first part contains 125 chapters and (b) the second part contains 82 chapters. It contains 18,000 verses. It describes topics such as liberation, religion, constellations, and philosophy, grammar, etymology, astrology, domestic advice, mantra-siddhi, Varnashrama-dharma, sacrifices, and prayascitta.

This text provides a summary of all 18 Puranas. The first part contains mantras and instructions on death, etc. in order. The story of the Ganga Avatara is also described in detail. The second part contains knowledge of the seven notes of music, the seven mandras of the saptaka, the middle and high positions of the notes, the murchanas, the pure and mixed tones, and the scale of music. This knowledge of musical patterns is still the basis of Indian music today. For those who are fascinated by Western music, it is noteworthy that until a few centuries after the Narada Purana, Western music only had five notes and the development of the musical scale was almost zero. The scales of music are based on the murchanas.

The Narada Purana is an important Hindu religious text, and one of the eighteen major Puranas accepted by Hindus. It is written from the viewpoint of Narada, a Hindu spiritual figure, and dates back to at least 500 BCE.

The text is divided into two parts: the first is composed of thoughts and stories from Narada, and the second contains verses addressed by the sage to gods and mortals. It encapsulates the knowledge of vast areas of Hindu philosophy and theology, encompassing Vishnu, Shiva, Shakti and the avatars of Vishnu.

Narada Purana contains numerous stories and mantras. One of the most important stories is that of Prahlada, the divine son of demon king Hiranyakashipu. He chose to worship Lord Vishnu instead of his own father, despite Hiranyakashipu's attempts to prevent him. The story highlights the importance of devotion and surrender to Divinity.

The mantras held in the Narada Purana are chanted by devotees during various rituals and ceremonies. The mantras have the power to invoke the presence of various gods and goddesses, and also offer protection from bad luck and negative influences. Narada Purana includes special mantras for health and healing, protection, abundance, success, and many more.

Another important part of the Narada Purana is the lessons it teaches. These include the importance of dharma, karma, and the cycle of reincarnation. It also stresses the importance of living ethically, following the varnas Varna system, and keeping the principles of Ahimsa (non-violence) and Satya (truthfulness).

The Narada Purana provides a spiritual gateway for Hindus to desire liberation through right action and right knowledge. It guides devotees to understand the power of mantra and to follow the rules of dharma and karma. It also teaches followers to keep their minds focused and their hearts full of love for all living beings.

Overall, the Narada Purana provides powerful guidance for devoted Hindus. It contains stories, mantras, and lessons that can help followers of Hinduism to understand the power of devotion, the importance of ethical living, and the principle of spiritual growth.

CHAPTER TWELVE

Garuda Purana

The Garuda Maha Purana is an ancient Vedic text believed to have been written around the beginning of the Common Era. It contains a wide range of information from descriptions of celestial spheres and astronomical phenomena to rules for proper governance and even mantras for various religious ceremonies. One main lesson contained in this scripture is the importance of forces beyond our realm—in this case through an emphasis on Vishnu, Shiva, and other deities—along with their respective mantras. In doing so, it teaches that complete surrender to these forces is necessary for anyone's well-being. This resonates with Hindu philosophy in general, as many Hindus believe in divine guidance flowing through special scriptures like this one. Ultimately, the Garuda Maha Purana has much wisdom concealed within its pages which can be studied and applied in order to help lead a better life.

The Garuda Maha Purana consists of two parts - the Garuda Purana proper and the Agni-Tantra, which includes teachings on ritual worship and ritual fire sacrifices. The Garuda Purana proper focuses on teachings related to the Bhagavad Gita, Ayurveda, Kriya Yoga, the Upanishads and

Vedanta. In particular, it focuses on the essential spiritual truths of the Advaita Vedanta school of thought, which emphasizes the idea of the unity of all souls, the underlying reality of the Divine and the core ethical values and principles of the Hindu way of life.

The Garuda Purana is also appreciated for its insights into various mantras, an important part of Hindu ritual practice. It contains various 'Bija' mantras, or one-word statements that are believed to be powerful enough to invoke the gods. It also includes various other mantras which individuals can recite in order to seek spiritual protection and divine guidance. The mantras are believed to come from the primordial energy, and can be used for emotional healing and spiritual unfoldment.

The lessons of the Garuda Maha Purana are about achieving harmony and unity through living an ethical life based on the foundational principles of truth, purity, inner peace and compassion. The text also stresses the importance of spiritual practices, such as meditation and the recitation of mantras, in order to cultivate greater self-awareness and spiritual insight.

In addition to its teachings, the Garuda Maha Purana also provides insight into many of the rituals and ceremonies associated with Hinduism, including the worship of the gods and goddesses, the observance of fasts and festivals, and festivals celebrating the birth of Rama and Saraswati. The text is also an invaluable resource for those seeking to understand the doctrines and theological beliefs of the Hindu faith, in particular, the Advaita Vedanta doctrine.

The Vishnu Purana is an ancient text with Vishnu as its narrator and Garuda as its listener. It describes the worship of Vishnu and is divided into two parts, the first containing 229 chapters and 18,000 verses, and the second containing 279 chapters and 18,000 verses. The first part is considered to be cosmogonic in nature.

The Garuda Purana contains detailed descriptions of post-mortem events, the netherworld, the Yamaloka, the Naraka, and the 84 lakh Yonis in the form of hellish lives. It also contains descriptions of many Suryavanshi and Chandravanshi kings. People usually shy away from reading this text as it is traditionally read after someone's death. In reality, this Purana contains a scientific description of the fetus in the womb after death, referred to as Vaitarani River, etc. At that time, there was no scientific knowledge about the development of the fetus in all of Europe.

Overall, the Garuda Maha Purana is an important and inspirational source of guidance for anyone seeking to lead a truly spiritual life based on the values and principles of the Hindu faith. Its teachings are timeless and encompass the core spiritual truths of the Advaita Vedanta, emphasizing the importance of living an ethical life and engaging in spiritual practices, such as meditation and mantra recitation.

CHAPTER THIRTEEN

Kurma Purana

The Kurma Purana is one of the oldest scriptures in Hinduism. It contains a variety of stories, hymns and mantras that focus on the worship of Lord Vishnu and His various incarnations. The main purpose of this Purana is to explain how creation comes about as a result of divine actions taken by Lord Vishnu in many different forms. This scripture also speaks about the various qualities associated with God, such as knowledge, strength, intelligence and more. Additionally, it offers lessons for attaining spiritual enlightenment and achieving harmony in life. For example, it includes mantras to invoke peace and blessings from the gods and goddesses such as Siva, Devi Parvati and Ganesha. Furthermore, it emphasizes living a life governed by Dharma or virtue so as to achieve ultimate happiness and liberation from all suffering.

The Kurma Purana is a Hindu holy text, believed to have been written in the 2nd century CE. It is named after Kurma, the Avatar of Vishnu, and describes the origins, geography, and religious festivals of India and the nature of the outside world. It includes a section on the Ramayana, Mahabharata, Prithvi Sukta, the ten incarnations of Vishnu, stories of the blessed ones, the genealogy of the gods, the battle of

Kurukshetra, and the story of the churning of the cosmic ocean.

The Kurma Purana is composed of ten thousand verses, divided into six sections. It begins with an introduction to the four Vedic priests, and their privileged access to the divine knowledge. This leads to a description of creation, and the divine energies of Brahma, Vishnu, and Shiva. In the second section, the Purana tells the story of the churning of the ocean of milk and the birth of gods and planets. This story of cosmic creation explains the origins of the material world. The third section is devoted to the devotional path, and it highlights the importance of chanting mantras and worshipping the divine.

The fourth section of the Kurma Purana begins with a discussion on the observance of fasts, and the performance of yagnas. It also includes stories of gods and goddess like Shiva, Vishnu, and Krishna, and their devotees. The fifth section explains the nature of material enjoyment and the rules of Dharma. It also contains rules of conduct and spiritual guidance. The sixth and final section is devoted to the ten avatars of Vishnu and how their influences have shaped the history of India.

The Kurma Purana provides spiritual guidance and moral lessons for anyone searching for a higher purpose in life. Some of the significant lessons from the Purana include: practicing Dharma and self-control, remaining steadfast in one's spiritual path, striving for truth, and remaining devoted to God. The Kurma Purana also contains various mantras and prayers to attain spiritual liberation. Some of the most important mantras for gaining the grace of God include Vishnu Mantra, Shiva Mantra, Rama Mantra, Vishnu Gayatri mantra, and the Mahamrityunjaya Mantra.

The Kurma Purana describes the avatar of Vishnu. It consists of four samhitas - (a) Brahmani, (b) Bhagavati, (c) Saur and (d) Vaishnavi. Only the Brahmani samhita is available today. It contains 6,000 shlokas, divided into two parts with 51 and 44 chapters respectively. It also contains the five characteristics of a Purana, including the Isha-Gita and Vyasa-Gita. It is believed to have been composed in the 6th century.

The Kurma Purana consists of 18,000 shlokas and four khandas. It provides a concise summary of the four Vedas. It also provides a detailed account of the Samudra Manthan, the avatar of Kurma, related to Vishnu. It also describes the creation of Brahma, Shiva, Vishnu, the Earth, the Ganges, the four Yugas, the four ashrams of human life, and the Chandravanshi kings.

CHAPTER FOURTEEN

Skanda Purana

The Skanda Purana is an ancient Hindu text and contains a vast variety of topics within its verses. It centers around the stories of LordSkanda, son of Lord Shiva and Parvati, with the main focus on highlighting his heroic accomplishments during the battle with demons. The chapters are often filled with mantras dedicated to Lord Skanda while also containing genealogical information regarding various gods, goddesses, and kings who lived at different times in history. Additionally, there are many lessons that can be learnt from this scripture such as staying true to your values and avoiding desire for wealth or power. Finally, due to its age (over 1,500 years) numerous mantras are found throughout skanda puranas which emphasizes it's importance as a spiritual text for Hindus all over the world.

The Skanda Purana is named after the son of Shiva, Skanda (Kartikeya, Subrahmanya). It is the largest of the Puranas, containing 81,000 verses in two parts. It contains six samhitas - Sanatkumara, Suta, Shanka, Vaishnava, Brahma, and Saur. Madhvacharya wrote an extensive commentary called Tatparya-dipika on the Suta Samhita. The end of this samhita also contains two songs - the Brahma Gita (Chapter 12) and the Suta Gita (Chapter 8).

The Skanda Purana is the largest of the Puranas, containing 81,000 verses and six sections. It is a detailed description of ancient India, including the 27 constellations, 18 rivers, the beauty of the Arunachal Pradesh, the 12 Jyotirlingas located in India, and the description of the Ganges descent. It also mentions the Syahadri mountain range and the Kanya Kumari temple. This Purana also contains the allegorical story of the origin of Soma Deva, the stars, and their son, Budha Graha.

Skanda Purana is one of the most influential and important Hindu religious texts, belonging to the group of eighteen major Puranas. It is considered to be an authoritative source of knowledge, providing a comprehensive description of the nature and purpose of Hindu religious life. In the Skanda Purana, there is an entire section dedicated to the glory of Shiva and the worship of him, known as the Shivasamhita.

At its core, the Skanda Purana presents a philosophical discourse about the path of liberation and the way to ultimate fulfillment. It propounds the theory of karma and the law of karma-yoga — the practice of selfless action — as the means of attaining the Divine grace. The texts also offer an elaborate description of various forms of worship, provide guidance on how to perform rituals, and include numerous mantras. These are designed to evoke the power of the gods or to create a successful ritual experience.

The primary message of the Skanda Purana is that material wealth and worldly desires should be eschewed in favor of leading a spiritually fulfilling life. The text emphasizes that the path of devotion and bhakti to god is the most auspicious one, and encourages the reader to develop a close relationship with the divine. In addition, it encourages generosity, forbearance, and forms of agnihotra, or fire offerings.

The Skanda Purana also serves as an important resource for mantras and their proper recitation. Each deity has their own mantra and the text contains many mantras that are dedicated to specific gods or goddesses. For example, the Shiva Gayatri Mantra is a powerful mantra associated with the worship of Shiva, while the eight-syllabled Dakshinamurti Mantra is dedicated to the god Dakshinamurti. Other important mantras featured in the Skanda Purana include the Purusha Sukta, which is chanted in many rituals, and the Saraswati Mantra, used for invoking knowledge and learning.

It is clear from the Skanda Purana that the path of devotion to God, ritual offerings, and mantras are essential components of Hindu religious life. The text provides guidance for those who wish to approach the gods for blessings, and communicates a powerful message of seeking liberation from the cycle of birth and death and attaining divine grace. The incredible depth and breadth of the texts remind us of the importance and power of spiritual connection and the devotion one should have for the divine.

CHAPTER FIFTEEN

Vamana Purana

The Vamana Purana is a rich religious text associated with the Vaishnavism Hindu tradition. It contains stories, teachings and mantras that are used for worship, meditation and spiritual enlightenment. The Purana is composed of eighteen thousand verses and mainly focuses on Lord Vishnu in his five forms: Kurma, Varaha, Narasimha, Vamana and Parashurama. It also outlines an array of Vedic ceremonies such as baptism; describes a plethora of deities including some from other religions; provides directions for daily rituals; instructs on pious activities such as charity to produce positive karma; advises its readers on how to navigate through life ethically with dharma; and explains mantras devoted to various gods and goddesses. Overall, the Vamana Purana offers useful insights into spiritual understanding as well as practical advice applicable to our daily lives.

The Vamana Purana contains 95 chapters and 10,000 verses, divided into two parts. The first part describes the avatar of Vishnu in detail, which took place in Bharuchchch (Gujarat). In addition to this, the text also includes the creation of the seven dvipas, the geographical features of the earth, the important mountains, rivers, and divisions of

India.

The Vamana Purana is one of the 18 major Hindu Puranas, which is believed to have been composed by Veda Vyasa in the form of a dialogue between two sages, Devarupa and Brighu. The text draws from a variety of religious and philosophical concepts from Hinduism, such as creation theories, cosmologies, ancient traditions, and Vedic mantras. It is believed to have been composed between 500 BCE and 300 CE, although some scholars propose that the text was actually composed at a later date.

The Vamana Purana is believed to have originally been composed of ten volumes with a total of 28,000 shlokas, although the current version only contains three volumes with a total of about 10,000 shlokas. These three volumes consist of Vamana-Savarni-Samhita, Uttarardha, and the Bhagavatottara Purana.

The Vamana Purana is dedicated to Lord Vishnu, who is described as being the original source of cosmic energy. The text also includes stories and legends about various Hindu gods and goddesses, including Shiva and Parvati, Ganesha, and Rama. Much of the text is dedicated to a thorough description of Vishnu's avatars, including some of his most famous incarnations such as Rama, Krishna, and Vamana. The text also contains stories and teachings of the ancient sages and ascetics, such as Valmiki, Markandeya, and Vasishtha.

The Vamana Purana is more than just an ancient religious text; it is an essential part of Hindu philosophy and an invaluable source of spiritual knowledge. Written in an easy-to-follow style, it is rich with stories and teachings that offer readers valuable insights into the various gods and goddesses of Hinduism as well as an understanding of the importance of mantras and their spiritual applications. Ultimately, the teachings and lessons of Vamana Purana can be used to cultivate greater understanding, peace, and harmony in one's life.

There is one famous story about Vishu's Vamana Avatar - Mahabali, the demon king, was renowned for his generosity and benevolence, and his rule was likened to a golden era. Legend has it that Mahabali defeated the gods and took control of the three worlds, prompting the gods to ask Lord Vishnu for help in their fight against the demon king. However, as Mahabali was a devotee of Lord Vishnu, the god found it difficult to take sides. Vishnu then took on the form of Vamana, a poor Brahmin, and visited Mahabali. He asked for property rights over a piece of land that measured three paces, to which Mahabali agreed.

Vamana then grew in size and covered everything the king ruled in just two steps. To keep his word and honour, Mahabali offered his head for the third step, thus making Onam a celebration of his generosity and benevolence.

Finally, the Vamana Purana contains several powerful mantras and verses that are used as part of rituals or daily meditation. These mantras are believed to have powerful healing, protective, and spiritual properties. As such, they are used in many Hindu- and Buddhist-related religious ceremonies.

THIRD GROUP

The third category consists of the Matsya Purana, Agni Purana, Linga Purana, Brahmanda Purana, Markandeya Purana, Brahma Vaivarta Purana, Brahma Purana, and Bhavisya Purana. This group is mainly concerned with detailing the creation of the universe, the development of Hinduism and Indian culture, and proper conduct for Hindus.

CHAPTER SIXTEEN

Matsya Purana

The Matsya Purana is an ancient Indian text which strives to help its readers understand the events of the creation of the world. It also serves as a significant religious and spiritual resource, filled with teachings, lessons, mantras and stories meant to guide one on the spiritual path. This book contains details about time cycles, mythology about gods, kings and their wars and discourses between God Vishnu and wise sages. Additionally, it provides insights into some of life's biggest questions like the purpose of life, good and bad karma, meditation, yoga among other essential practices that should be followed by believers in order to lead an ethical lifestyle. Devoted followers of this Purana can gain knowledge from various verses in Sanskrit which cover topics like Hindu theology as well as metaphysical philosophy. Lastly, through meditating upon these sacred mantras one can find peace within oneself ultimately leading to spiritual growth.

The Matsya Purana is an ancient Indian Hindu text that is part of the eighteen Mahapuranas, which are part of the corpus of Hindu scriptures. Primarily, it tells the story of the birth of Vishnu in his fish avatar, and the divergent roles of man and the gods who created him to protect the universe during the great flood.

It is believed to have been composed by Veda Vyasa. The main theme of the text is the destruction of the universe by a great flood and the rebirth of the world afterwards. The contents of the Purana consist of cosmology, Manu's instructions, genealogy of famous kings, sages, temples and holy places, sacred rivers, legendary battles and their invokers, animals and birds, gods and goddesses. It also contains lessons on Dharma and yogic meditation.

One of the main lessons that Matsya Purana contains is the need to lead a moral life in order to gain ultimate liberation. It provides a spiritual message reminding us to recognize our place as part of the macrocosm, to be aware of the great cycle of cause and effect, and to strive for peace and harmony. The Purana also speaks concerning the interrelatedness of all beings as part of a great cycle of life, as well as the need for meditation and contemplation for peace and harmony.

The Matsya Purana also contains many mantras, or hymns, that are used in Hindu rituals. Many of these mantras are used in offerings to the gods, in ceremonies conducted during the festivals, or for protection against illnesses and other misfortunes. Some of the most popular mantras include the Vishnu Sahasranama, the Purusha Sukta, the Rudram, and the Ashtakam prayer.

The Matsya Purana contains 290 chapters and 14,000 verses. This text provides a detailed description of the avatar of Matsya. It also chronicles the history of all the planets, four yugas, and the Chandravanshi kings in our solar system. Fascinating stories of Kashyapa, Devayani, Sharmishtha, and King Yayati are also found in this Purana. It is believed to have been composed in the third century.

The Matsya Purana is characterized by five distinct features: it contains 290 chapters, 14,000 verses, 19,000 verses in the ancient versions, a description of the great flood, and a list of kings of the Kali Yuga. It is an invaluable source of knowledge, providing insight into the ancient Indian culture and mythology.

In conclusion, the Matsya Purana is an ancient Hindu text that tells the story of the great flood, and contains many lessons and mantras to be used in different rituals. It emphasizes the need to lead a moral life and the interrelatedness of all creation, as well as providing Dharma teachings. The mantras it includes have been used in Hindu rituals for centuries and are still used to this day.

CHAPTER SEVENTEEN

Agni Purana

The Agni Purana is an ancient Hindu scripture, estimated to have been composed between 400 and 1000 CE. The main focus of the text is on Vedic mantras, rituals, and hymns, as well as on numerous topics related to cosmology and mythology. It consists of roughly 15,000 verses, including topics such as cyclic time, sacred geography and mountains, philosophical systems like karma and samsara (reincarnation), dharma (duty and morality), meditation practices like pranayama (breath control), astrology and planetary sciences. Additionally, it includes mantras chanted by various rishis or sages in order to propitiate gods like Agni (the god of fire) or Indra (the god of storm). The Agni Purana also describes a variety of yantras - inscribed diagrams used for rituals - associated with different deities or aspects of cosmic energy. This is a valuable source for understanding the potentially wide range of ritual activities which were once practiced in the Hindu tradition.

Agni Purana is one of the 18 major Hindu religious texts known as the Puranas. It is among the oldest of the Puranas, estimated to have been composed between the 2nd and 4th centuries CE, though much of its material may come from much earlier sources. Agni Purana contains a wealth of information concerning Vedic beliefs and practices. It is divided into 17 sections and is composed of over 15,000 verses in total.

At its core, Agni Purana contains mantras and rituals related to the god Agni (the god of fire). Verses from Agni Purana are recited during sacrifices and during many other religious occasions. The text also contains information about other gods and goddesses, such as Surya (the sun god), Shiva, and Vishnu. The Purana also includes information about religious karma, epics, and various forms of medicine.

The Agni Purana has sections devoted to certain topics, such as sacred mantras and descriptions of meetings between Devas and Rishis. The mantras are composed mostly in Vedic Sanskrit and are used to worship the gods and goddesses mentioned in the text. They are often accompanied by mantras from other Vedic works, such as the Upanishads, Mahabharata, Ramayana and Bhagavad Gita.

The Rishis who figure prominently in the Agni Purana are a group of seers and wise men who are believed to have composed, organized, and recited Vedic hymns and mantras. They are the traditional authors of all of the Vedic texts, and their knowledge was seen as a direct gift from the gods. The Agni Purana devotes significant sections to the Rishis and their teachings.

The Agni Purana—its narrator is Agni and its listener is Vashishtha. This is why it is called the Agni Purana. It is considered to be a great repository of Indian culture and knowledge. It also contains descriptions of Shiva Linga, Durga, Ganesh, Surya, Pranaprathista, and many other topics such as geography, mathematics, astrology, marriage, death, Shakunavidya, Vastuvidya, daily rituals, political science, warfare, Dharma Shastra, Ayurveda, music, poetry, grammar, and cosmogony.

Agni Purana - This ancient text covers a wide range of topics, from the geography of Mithila (Bihar and the surrounding states) to cultural history, politics, the educational system, iconography, taxation theories, army organization, theories on the right reasons to wage war, diplomacy, local laws, the construction of public projects, water distribution techniques, trees and plants, medicine, Vastu Shastra (architecture), gemology, grammar, metrics, poetry, food, rituals, and more.

The Agni Purana contains 383 chapters and 15,000 verses, making it a veritable encyclopedia of Indian culture. This text contains condensed versions of Matsyavatar, Ramayana, and Mahabharata. In addition, it contains conversations on various topics such as Dharmaveda, Gandharvaveda, and Ayurveda, which are also known as Upavedas.

In conclusion, the Agni Purana is an ancient and incredibly important Hindu religious text. It contains mantras, rituals and information about various gods, but is primarily focused on Agni and the Rishis. It is one of the most read and studied Puranas today, and features prominently in the rituals and ceremonies of Hinduism.

CHAPTER EIGHTEEN

Linga Purana

The Linga Purana is one of the eighteen major Hindu Puranas that combine mythology, cosmology, and philosophy. It details the creation of the universe from aShivalinga, which then splits outward into various forms and aspects. The text emphasizes the importance of Shiva to religious practice and provides detailed instructions for worship and rituals related to him. It also outlines a number of mantras associated with Shiva, including invocations for protection, healing, and spiritual growth. Many of these mantras emphasize qualities such as courage, patience, wisdom, gratitude, humility and surrender before the divine power of God. Linga Purana offers lessons that provide wisdom on how to conduct moral living in order to reach higher stages—enlightenment or liberation—in life. Those who follow these instructions will eventually be rewarded with rewards from Ishwara as a result of their devotion in performing regular pooja (ritual) towards Shiva.

The Linga Purana is a Hindu religious text that details the origin of the universe, the origin of the gods, and the origins of other sacred forms associated with the religion. It is a part of the larger Purana literature, which is a corpus of Vedic scriptures. The Linga Purana is distinct from other works in that it does not make much reference to any other scripture. It is dedicated to the god Shiva and so is an important source for Shiva worshippers.

One of the major topics of the Linga Purana is creation. The text describes how Shiva created the universe from the primordial fire and manifested himself in a linga, an iconic representation of his power. The linga is associated with the base concepts of connectivity and creation, as it is the physical representation of the unity of all things. The Purana goes on to explain the duties of a Brahma devotee which include keeping the linga clean, adorning it with flowers and performing Puja rituals.

The Linga Purana also contains mantras and instructions for worshipping Shiva. In it, Shiva is described as the lord of lords, the bestower of all boons, and the ruler of the universe. Other passages offer explanations of Shiva's attributes and the importance of worshipping him. The text also includes instructions on meditating on the linga in order to foster inner peace.

The Linga Purana also explains the benefits of performing Puja rituals and the importance of maintaining a state of devotion to Shiva. Through this, one can achieve harmony and peace of mind. Additionally, the text emphasizes the need to stay away from vices and to strive for the realization of one's spiritual goals.

The importance of devotion and meditation is also stressed throughout the Linga Purana, as it can bring about connection with the divine and inner peace. The text also discusses various philosophical concepts and ideas, such as how we are all interconnected and how our connection to the divine is an important part of our journey.

The Linga Purana is a description of the worship of Lord Shiva. It contains stories of Shiva's 28 avatars and 11,000 shlokas and 163 chapters. It is divided into two parts, the Purva and the Uttara. It is believed to have been composed in the 8th-9th century. This scripture does not rest on the traditional Puranic characteristics.

The Linga Purana contains a list of the creation of the universe, the Yugas, Kalpas, etc. in the period of creation. The story of King Ambarisha is also written in this scripture. It also mentions the Agni mantras and Agni Vidya in detail.

In conclusion, the Linga Purana is an important religious text in Hinduism and contains important teachings and mantras related to Shiva. The text explains Shiva's origin and his importance, as well as the benefits of worshipping him and performing Puja rituals. It also emphasizes the importance of maintaining a state of devotion and meditating on the linga in order to come closer to the divine and reach inner peace.

CHAPTER NINETEEN

Brahmanda Purana

Brahmanda Purana is an ancient Indian scripture from the Vedic tradition. It belongs to one of the 18 major Puranas and contains a compilation of teachings, mantras, and deities. One of its main themes is about universal creation which is described as a "cosmic egg" created by the Hindu god Brahma. It also contains information on cosmology, astrology, geography and other theological topics. Additionally it provides an in-depth look at various aspects of spiritual life including worship, meditation, spiritual powers and liberation through renunciation. It also serves as a guide to living with righteousness that takes into account physical, mental and spiritual development. As such it outlines mantras which provide moral guidance as well as blessings for success in worldly actions while still emphasising restraint in dealings with material objects. In essence Brahmanda Purana is an invaluable source of wisdom containing lessons applicable to both modern times and timeless truths pertaining to the universe itself.

The Brahmanda Purana is an ancient Hindu text that dates back to the 3rd century BC. It is one of the eighteen major Puranas, and is considered an important source of knowledge about Hindu mythology, philosophy, and cultural history. The Purana is divided into twelve khandas, or sections, and is composed of varying material including stories, dialogues, hymns, proverbs, ritual instructions, and philosophical speculations.

The first khanda of the Brahmanda Purana is devoted to the creation of the cosmos. It details the processes involved in the creation of the universe and the various gods, goddesses, and creatures found within it. It provides an explanation of the fundamental laws of nature, including the three gunas (sattva, rajas, and tamas), the importance of dharma and karma, and the origin of the avatara forms of Vishnu. The khanda also contains stories about the birth and life of Brahma and Vishnu, as well as the creation of the four Veda.

The second khanda of the Brahmanda Purana is mostly focused on Shiva and the Vedic gods. It provides detailed accounts of the many forms of Shiva, Vishnu, and Brahma, and their roles within the cosmic system. It contains stories about Shiva's many avatara, such as the much beloved Hanuman, as well as the various incarnations of Vishnu, such as Rama and Krishna. The khanda also contains stories of the devas and asuras, as well as the Mahabharata war, the Mahapralaya, and the many battles fought by the gods.

The third khanda focuses on the people living in the Bharata Varsha, or the subcontinent of India. It provides detailed descriptions of the various states, provinces, rivers, and mountains that make up India. It also contains stories of the great kings, heroes, sages, and yogis, as well as accounts of their various adventures. A variety of mantras and hymns are also found within this khanda, and can be used to invoke the various gods and goddesses found in the Hindu pantheon.

The Brahmanda Purana carries a number of important lessons and teachings. Through its stories and dialogues, it encourages the application of dharma and the balancing of one's three gunas. It also teaches the importance of spiritual practice, the performance of righteous deeds, and the consequences of bad karma. Ultimately, the Brahmanda Purana is a source of both knowledge and wisdom, and its contents can be used to gain insight into the mysteries and wonders of the cosmos.

The Brahmanda Purana is an ancient Sanskrit text composed of 10,900 verses and 109 chapters. It is divided into four parts: (1) Prakriya, (2) Anushanga, (3) Upodghata, and (4) Upasamhara. It is believed to have been composed between 400 and 600 CE.

It is believed that the Adhyatma Ramayana, now a separate text, was originally a part of the Brahmanda Purana. This text contains descriptions of the planets located in the universe, as well as the histories of many Suryavanshi and Chandravanshi kings. It also provides an account of the seven Manvantaras, or eras, from the time of creation to the present. Additionally, the story of Parashurama is also included in this Purana. It can be considered the world's first cosmological treatise. The knowledge of this Purana was even taken to Indonesia, as evidenced by the presence of Sanskrit words in the Indonesian language.

CHAPTER TWENTY

Markandeya Purana

Markandeya Purana is an ancient Hindu text from India. It's believed to have been written between 400-1000 AD, and contains stories about the gods, Rishi's (Hindu saints), as well as explanations of Hindu philosophy and mysticism. The Purana also explains various kinds of religious rituals, along with mantras to be chanted for various occasions. One interesting story from the Purana tells of a special protective mantra that grants eternal life; it was used by Markandeya, thus giving the text its name. In addition to spiritual teachings, Markandeya Purana can also be seen as a kind of moral lesson book full of tales that teach important values like humility, compassion, self-sacrifice and honesty. This very influential masterpiece still acts a guide today for many Hindus seeking to know more about their faith and traditions.

The Markandeya Purana is considered one of the oldest scriptures. It contains descriptions of Vedic deities such as Indra, Agni, and Surya. Its narrator is Markandeya Rishi and its listener is Kroushtuki Shishya.It describes topics such as household duties, rituals, daily activities, regular duties, vows, festivals, stories of devoted wives, yoga, and Durga-mahatmya.

In comparison to other scriptures, the Markandeya Purana is relatively small, containing only 9,000 verses and 137 chapters. This text includes conversations between Rishimarkandeya and Rishi Jamini on topics such as social justice and yoga. Additionally, it contains stories related to Goddess Durga and Lord Krishna.

The Markandeya Purana is an ancient Sanskrit text which is a part of the major eighteen Puranas. It is an important scripture and is believed to have been composed during the Vedic period, and believed to have been in existence for over 5000 years. It derives its name from the sage Markandeya, who wrote it during his time.

The primary subject of the teachings in the Purana is about the glory of Lord Vishnu and Devi Parvati, and in particular the relation between Lord Shiva and Devi Parvati.

The Markandeya Purana is made up of three chapters (or 'Kandas') and is divided into two sections. The first part (known as the Uttar Kanda) consists of 271 chapters, and deals primarily with stories, legends, and teachings related to Lord Vishnu and Devi Parvati.

The second part (known as the Purva Kandha) consists of 101 chapters, and contains spiritual and moral discourses related to creation, devotional service, and the different paths of worship.

The Markandeya Purana is packed with insights and wisdom, and conveys a range of inspiring stories and useful lessons. Some of the teachings it contains are the importance of charity, the value of devotion, the power of prayer, and the need for righteousness and justice.

The Purana also contains numerous mantras, which can be chanted to gain spiritual knowledge and even to help one to reach their destination. Some of the most popular mantras include the Surya Mantra, the Durga Mantra, the Vishnu Mantra, the Lakshmi Mantra, and the Mahalakshmi Mantra.

In addition to the mantras, the Purana also provides guidance on a range of topics, from personal health and self-awareness to statecraft. In each of these topics, the Markandeya Purana offers powerful and useful advice.

In summary, the Markandeya Purana is one of the most important and influential scriptures of Hinduism. It contains a wealth of knowledge, stories, lessons and mantras that can be used to gain spiritual knowledge and develop faith. Its teachings can be considered timeless, and its mantras are still chanted by devotees today.

CHAPTER TWENTY-ONE

Brahma Vaivarta Purana

The Brahma Vaivarta Purana is an ancient Indian religious text filled with lessons and mantras that was believed to have been written in the 4th century C.E. This book contains stories about various Hindu deities, along with various teachings said to be imparted by Vishnu himself. The main theme of this Purana is the return of Radha or Sita as Vishnu's beloved consort, thus making it part of the Bhakti literature; however, it also contains numerous other faith related topics. It features various mantras and prayers meant to invoke mercy and grace from Lord Vishnu or Krishna, while also providing practical advice on how to peacefully traverse life's many hardships. More recently, some spiritual leaders cite parts of this text as examples for a god-centric devotion within modern society.

The Brahmavaivarta Purana is a Vaishnavite scripture that describes the character of Shri Krishna. It contains a total of 18,000 shlokas and is divided into four sections: (a) Brahma, (b) Prakriti, (c) Ganesh, and (d) Shri Krishna-Janma.

The Brahmavaivarta Purana is comprised of 18,000 shlokas and 218 chapters. This text glorifies the greatness of Brahma, Ganesh, Tulsi, Savitri, Lakshmi, Saraswati, and Krishna, and includes stories related to them. It also contains knowledge related to Ayurveda.

The Brahma Vaivarta Purana is an ancient Indian scriptures composed in Sanskrit. It is an important part of the Hindu epic Mahabharata and is one of the seventeen Mahapuranas. It contains a variety of stories, legends, and teachings related to Hinduism. It is considered an important source of Hindu mythology, mythology from the Puranic period of Indian history (early centuries CE).

The text focuses mainly on the stories of Krishna and Radha, two main characters from the epic Mahabharata. It presents their early romantic relationship and their later parenthood, ultimately displaying their playful and spiritual bond. Besides their stories, the text also contains stories of other gods and goddesses, such as Rama and Shiva, and various other figures.

The text is structured around thirty-three chapters, which cover various themes and topics. These topics include the origin and evolution of the world and its inhabitant, tales of divine figures such as Krishna and Vishnu, stories of creation and destruction, rules of morality, various supplementary tales, and rules pertaining to rituals, festivals, and so on.

While the stories in the text facilitate an understanding of Hindu ideologies, the teachings presented in the detail many lessons that are applicable in daily life. These lessons include discipline, moderation, contentment, patience, diligence, and acceptance of others. Through tales of divine figures, the text also presents mantras that can be repeated for spiritual healing and contentment. A few of these mantras can be found in the Bhagavat Gita, and is sung as part of Sanskrit chanting.

The Brahma Vaivarta Purana contains various teachings, tales, and mantras that have inspiring and spiritual aspects. Its stories provide an insight into the culture and beliefs of the part of Indian culture. It presents timeless lessons and mantras that are relevant to all people regardless of their religion or spiritual beliefs. It is a classic text that encourages reflection and provides valuable lessons for all its readers.

CHAPTER TWENTY-TWO

Brahma Purana

The Brahm Purana is also known as the Adi Purana. It is mentioned in all the ancient scriptures. It contains a varying number of verses, ranging from 10,000 to 12,000 and 13,787. The discourse of this Purana was given by the sage Romaharshana in the Naimisharanya. It describes the creation, the origin of Manu, the description of his dynasty, the origin of the gods and the creatures. It also provides a detailed description of various pilgrimage sites. It has a total of 245 chapters. It also has a subsidiary, the Saura Upa Purana, which describes the Konark Sun Temple of Odisha.

The Brahma Purana is one of the oldest Puranas, containing 246 chapters and 14,000 verses. It includes descriptions of the creation of the universe, the genealogy of Manu, the dynasties of the gods and the creatures, the Ramayana, and the story of Krishna Avatar. It also includes descriptions of pilgrimages.

In addition to praising the greatness of Brahman, this scripture also includes accounts of the creation of the universe, the descent of the Ganges, the Ramayana, and the Krishna Avatar. Through this scripture, one can gain some knowledge of the creation of the universe and the civilization of the Indus Valley.

The Brahma Purana is a text that describes the planets of the universe. It includes the story of Parashurama, the genealogy of the Chandravanshi and Suryavanshi kings, and a description of their histories.

The Brahma Purana contains many stories about the creation of the universe and the stories of the many great deeds performed by Brahma and the various other gods and goddesses. This Purana also discusses various aspects of Dharma, rituals, and Sastra. rana consists of 1200 verses divided into three parts: the past, the present, and the future.

CHAPTER TWENTY-THREE

Bhavisya Purana

The Bhavishya Purana is an ancient Hindu scripture that contains stories, myths, and teachings pertaining to how the universe works and operates. It dates back to the Vedic period and its main focus is on the cyclical theme of life and death. It holds within it mantras which serve as a form of protection or blessing when read or uttered during auspicious occasions such as weddings or funerals. Additionally, it covers a variety of topics including karma and reincarnation, destiny, and morality. According to this scripture, every individual's life is determined by their past lives and actions; thus making it a central theme in many religious Hindu practices. Furthermore, it also contains various lessons to be learned from these stories that can provide insight into present day situations as well helping create one's spiritual path moving forward.

The Bhavishya Purana is a description of future events. It is divided into two parts: (a) the first part (Adhyaya 41) and (b) the second part (Adhyaya 171). It contains a total of 15,000 shlokas. There are five parvas in this text: (a) Brahmaparva, (b) Vishnuparva, (c) Shivaparva, (d) Suryaparva, and (e) Pratisargaparva. It mainly describes Brahman-dharma, achara, varnashrama-dharma, etc. It is believed to have been composed between 500 and 1200 CE.

The Bhavishya Purana contains 129 chapters and 28,000 shlokas. It discusses the importance of the Sun, the formation of the 12 months of the year, the social, religious, and educational regulations of India, and many other topics. It also provides important information about the identification of snakes, their venom, and their venomous parts. It also describes the stories of Vikram and Betal and the Betal Pachchisi. The story of Satya Narayan is also taken from this Purana.

The Bhavishya Purana is one of the most ancient Hindu texts, believed to be written by the great sage Ved Vyasa. The text is comprised of two major parts: the purvas (earlier books) and the uttaras (later books).

The Bhavishya Purana is said to record the past, present and future of the human race. The primary purpose of the text is to guide Hindus on how to conduct their lives in the present to ensure a better future. This ancient text contains prophecies and advice on many subjects such as Dharma (righteousness), Artha (wealth) and Kama (fulfillment of desires).

The Bhavishya Purana mainly focuses on predictions about the future of the world. It predicts the rise of great empires, of wise rulers, and of prosperous cities. It also forecasts many calamities, such as wars and famines, along with their respective remedies.

The Bhavishya Purana offers mantras and instructions to achieve success. It encourages Hindus to follow their dharma in all aspects of life, and to avoid wrongdoings. It also advises people to observe religious rites and rituals, to distribute wealth and charity, to partake in acts of kindness and mercy, to respect ancestral traditions and heritage, and to lead a disciplined life. In addition, the text encourages spiritual practices, such as chanting of specific hymns, performing meditations and other yogic practices.

In summary, the Bhavishya Purana is an invaluable source of ancient Hindu wisdom and knowledge. The text is a guide to leading a righteous life in the present, so as to ensure a prosperous future. It contains detailed advice about Dharmic principles, as well as mantras and instructions for achieving success and spiritual enlightenment.

Other Book Of The Author

1. The Moments When I Met God
2. Kashiyile Theertha Pathangal (Malayalam)
3. GURU GYAN VANI (Hindi)
4. Abhiprerak Gita (Hindi)
5. ASSI SE JAIN GHAT TAK (Hindi)
6. Hopelessness of Arjuna
7. The Soul and It's True Nature
8. Sense of Action (Karma)
9. Action through Wisdom
10. Action through Wisdom
11. THEORY AND PRACTICAL OF EVERY ACTION
12. LOGICAL UNDERSTANDING OF THE SUPREME
13. THE IMPERISHABLE SUPREME
14. Yatra Nishadraj se Hanuman Ghat Tak (Hindi)
15. Yatra Karnatak Ghat se Raja Ghat Tak (Hindi)
16. Yatra Pandey Ghat se Prayagraj Ghat Tak (Hindi)
17. Yatra Ranjendra Prasad Ghat se Dattatreya Ghat Tak (Hindi)
18. YaatraSindhiya Ghat se Gwaliar Ghat Tak (Hindi)
19. Yatra Mangala Gauri Ghat se Hanuman Gadhi Ghat Tak (Hindi)
20. Yatra Gaay Ghat Se Nishad Ghat Tak (Hindi)
21. MAA GANGA, GHATEN EVM UTSAV (Hindi)
22. Ganga Arti Dev Deepavali evam Any Utsav (Hindi)
23. Potentials of Digitalized India
24. VEDIC CONSCIOUSNESS
25. A Brief Introduction to Vedic Science
26. Kashi ke Barah Jyotirling (Hindi)
27. IMPACT OF MOTIVATION

28. Let's have a Milky Way Journey
29. Color Therapy in a Nutshell
30. Rigveda in a Nutshell
31. Yajurveda in a Nutshell
32. Samveda in a Nutshell
33. Atharva Veda in a Nutshell
34. Ayushman Bhava - Ayurveda
35. Srimad Bhagavad Gita and Upanishad Connection
36. Srimad Bhagavad Gita - an attempt to summarize each chapter.
37. Facts and Impact of Nakshatra
38. Astro Gems - NAVARATNA
39. Ekadashi - A Concise Overview
40. Nakshatraranyam
41. Inspirational Gita
42. A concise overview of Hanuman Chalisa.

Contact

DR. JAGADEESH PILLAI

PhD in Vedic Science

Four Times Guinness World Record Holder

Winner of Mahatma Gandhi Vishwa Shanti Puraskar and Global Peace Ambassador

Gemology, Astro & Vastu Consultant - Spiritual Counselor

Consultant for designing World Record Ideas

Efficient Tarot Card Reader

9839093003

myrichindia@gmail.com

drjagadeeshpillai@facebook

drjagadeeshpillai@instagram

jagadeeshpillai@youtube

www. JAGADEESHPILLAI.com

www.ingramcontent.com/pod-product-compliance
Lightning Source LLC
LaVergne TN
LVHW041131150826
845673LV00007B/2269